EXECUTIVE SUMMARY

The Islamic Republic of Iran is a theocratic republic with a Shia Islamic political system based on "velayat-e faqih" ("guardianship of the jurist" or "rule by the jurisprudent"). Shia clergy, most notably the "Rahbar" ("supreme jurisprudent" or "supreme leader") and political leaders vetted by the clergy dominated key power structures. While mechanisms for popular election existed within the structure of the state, the supreme leader held significant influence over the legislative and executive branches of government through unelected councils under his authority and held constitutional authority over the judiciary, the government-run media, and the armed forces. The supreme leader also indirectly controlled the internal security forces and other key institutions. Since 1989 the supreme leader has been Ayatollah Ali Khamenei. In 2013 voters elected Hassan Rouhani president who, on December 19, issued a 120 article Charter on Citizens' Rights. In the last parliamentary and Assembly of Experts elections held this year, candidate vetting by the unelected Guardian Council and restrictions on the media limited the freedom and fairness of these elections.

Civilian authorities maintained effective control over the security forces.

The most significant human rights (HR) problems were severe restrictions on civil liberties, including the freedoms of assembly, association, speech, religion, and press. Other HR problems included abuse of due process combined with use of capital punishment for crimes that do not meet the requirements of due process, as well as cruel, inhuman, or degrading treatment or punishment; and disregard for the physical integrity of persons, whom authorities arbitrarily and unlawfully detained, tortured, or killed.

Other reported human rights problems included politically motivated violence and repression; disappearances; limitations on citizens' ability to choose their government peacefully through free and fair elections. Of additional concern were harsh and life-threatening conditions in detention facilities, including lengthy solitary confinement, with instances of deaths in custody. Also of concern were arbitrary arrest and lengthy pretrial detention, sometimes incommunicado; continued impunity of the security forces; denial of fair public trial; the lack of an independent judiciary; arbitrary interference with privacy, family, home, and correspondence. Additionally there were severe restrictions on academic freedom; restrictions on freedom of movement; official corruption and lack of government transparency; constraints on investigations by international and nongovernmental organizations (NGOs) into alleged violations of human rights; legal and societal discrimination. There was also violence against women, ethnic and religious minorities, and lesbian, gay, bisexual, transgender, and intersex (LGBTI) persons. Lastly, there were significant HR problems with trafficking in persons and severe restrictions on the exercise of labor rights.

The government took few steps to investigate, prosecute, punish, or otherwise hold accountable officials, in the security services or elsewhere in government, who committed these abuses. Impunity remained pervasive throughout all levels of the government and security forces.

Section 1. Respect for the Integrity of the Person, Including Freedom from:

a. Arbitrary Deprivation of Life and other Unlawful or Politically Motivated Killings

The government and its agents reportedly committed arbitrary or unlawful killings, including, most commonly, by execution after arrest and trial without due process, or for crimes that did not meet the threshold of most serious crimes. The government made few and limited attempts to investigate allegations of deaths that occurred after or during reported torture or other physical abuse or after denying detainees medical treatment.

There were numerous reports that the government or its agents committed arbitrary or unlawful killings. According to unofficial reports, the government executed 469 persons by December 15, often after trials that did not adhere to basic principles of due process. These included individuals charged with crimes committed while under 18 years old. The government officially announced 114 executions by August, but it did not release further information for many, such as the dates of executions, the names of those executed, or the crimes for which they were executed.

The law provides for the death penalty in cases of murder, "attempts against the security of the state," "outrage against high-ranking officials," "moharebeh" (enmity towards or waging war against God or "drawing a weapon on the life, property, or chastity of persons or to cause terror as it creates the atmosphere of insecurity"), "fisad fil-arz" (corruption on earth--including apostasy or heresy), rape, adultery, drug possession and trafficking, recidivist alcohol use, consensual same-sex sexual activity, and "insults against the memory of Imam Khomeini (the previous supreme leader) and against the supreme leader of the Islamic Republic." Prosecutors frequently used moharebeh as a criminal charge against political dissidents and journalists, accusing them of struggling against the precepts of Islam and against the state, which upholds those precepts. Authorities have expanded the scope of this to include "working to undermine the Islamic establishment" and "cooperating with foreign agents or entities," according to academics. The judiciary is required to review and validate death sentences.

On August 2, the government executed 20 Iranian Sunni Kurds in Rajai Shahr prison, including Shahram Ahmadi for "enmity towards God." The International Campaign for Human Rights in Iran (ICHRI) reported Ahmadi was held in solitary confinement for 34 months of his sentence and executed based on a forced confession he had tried to appeal.

While the death sentence on charges of "corruption on earth" for spiritual leader Mohamed Ali Taheri was annulled in December 2015 and he was scheduled for release after serving a five-year sentence, new charges alleging his membership in a Marxist party were added on May 2. Although he was acquitted of all charges in June, he remained in prison at year's end on a hunger strike he began on September 30 protesting his detention. As of October 16, his family reportedly was not allowed to see him.

In his March 10 report to the UN Human Rights Council, Ahmed Shaheed, the UN Special Rapporteur on the situation of human rights in the Islamic Republic of Iran, reported that the penal code retained the death penalty for consensual same-sex sexual activity. According to Amnesty International (AI), Hassan Afshar, arrested in 2014 when he was 17 and charged with sodomy in July 2015, was executed by hanging on July 18.

Authorities carried out many executions in public. According to a September report by United Nations Secretary-General Ban Ki-moon, at least 10 executions were carried out publicly in the first six months of the year, including some in the presence of minors. NGO reports suggested that the actual figure was significantly higher.

There were also deaths in custody. Human Rights Activists News Agency (HRANA) reported that Nader Dastanpour died in custody at the Narmak 127 Police Station in Tehran after he and his brother were arrested in the morning of June 23. Dastanpour had visible signs of beating when he appeared before the Branch Seven Judicial Court judges, but authorities denied his request for a hospital transfer. He died several days later, according to his brother, after a cerebral hemorrhage caused by excessive beatings.

The penal code allows for the execution of juvenile offenders starting at age nine for girls and age 13 for boys. According to AI the government executed at least one juvenile offender, Hassan Afshar, on July 18. AI reported on October 11 that Zainab Sekaanvand, arrested at age 17 in 2012 for the murder of her husband, whom she had married at 15, was at risk of imminent execution.

Adultery remained punishable by death by stoning. According to the NGO Justice for Iran, provincial authorities have been ordered not to provide public information about stoning sentences since 2001. Justice for Iran reported there were two unnamed women sentenced to stoning in the past year, but there were no confirmed reports of death by stoning during the year.

Impunity for past unlawful killings continued. Family members of Sattar Beheshti, who died in police custody in 2012, were arrested on August 26 after visiting police and prison offices in Tehran to press for information about his death, according to HRANA.

b. Disappearance

There were reports of politically motivated abductions during the year attributed to government officials. The government made no effort to prevent or investigate such acts and punish those responsible. Plainclothes officials often seized journalists and activists without warning, and government officials refused to acknowledge custody or provide information on them. In other cases authorities held persons incommunicado for lengthy periods before permitting them to contact family members.

Hashem Zeinali, the father of missing student activist Saeed Zeinali, was sentenced to 91 days in prison and 74 lashes by the Tehran Criminal Court on February 22 for "disturbing the public order by participating in an illegal gathering," after he staged a protest at Evin Prison holding a photo of his missing son. Saeed Zeinali has been missing since his arrest in 1999 after student protests in Tehran. ICHRI Judiciary spokesman Gholamhossein Mohseni Ejei said in January, "so far no document has been found showing that [Saeed Zeinali] was arrested."

c. Torture and Other Cruel, Inhuman, or Degrading Treatment or Punishment

The constitution prohibits all forms of torture "for the purpose of extracting confession or acquiring information," but there were credible reports that security forces and prison personnel tortured and abused detainees and prisoners. Commonly reported methods of torture and abuse in prisons included prolonged solitary confinement or "white" torture, threats of execution or rape, forced virginity tests, sexual humiliation, sleep deprivation, electroshock, burnings, the use of pressure positions, and severe and repeated beatings. Human rights organizations, including Iran Human Rights, reported that authorities also used denial of medical care as a form of punishment for prisoners.

Some prison facilities, including Evin Prison in Tehran and Rajai Shahr Prison in Karaj, were notorious for the use of cruel and prolonged torture of political opponents of the government, particularly Wards 209 and Two of Evin Prison, which were reportedly controlled by the IRGC. Authorities also allegedly maintained unofficial secret prisons and detention centers outside the national prison system where abuse reportedly occurred.

Judicially sanctioned corporal punishment included flogging, blinding, and amputation, which the government defended as "punishment," not torture. According to Iran Human Rights, authorities amputated four fingers of the right hands of Faramarz and Majid Bigham on December 25 as punishment for their 2011 robbery convictions. Under the penal code, 149 offenses are punishable by flogging. According to Reporters Without Borders, journalist Mohammad Reza Fathi was sentenced to 459 lashes for "defamation" and "publishing false information" on April 13 in Saveh for his writings about local government officials. Media reported on May 27 that 30 students were arrested and given 99 lashes each for attending a mixed gender gathering in Qazvin where women were not dressed in legally required attire and members of the party were "dancing and jubilating" together. International media reported that authorities blinded a man on November 8 as punishment for assaulting a child in a 2009 acid attack that left her blind.

Prison and Detention Center Conditions

Prison conditions reportedly were often harsh and life threatening. Prisoner hunger strikes in protest of their treatment were common. Prisoners were often denied adequate medical treatment. Overcrowding was a problem. Refugee detainees were sometimes held in separate facilities and in some cases deported.

<u>Physical Conditions</u>: Overcrowding remained a problem in prisons with many prisoners forced to sleep on floors, in hallways, or in prison yards. HRANA reported that Mahabad Prison housed 700 prisoners, while its capacity was only 400.

Authorities occasionally held pretrial detainees with convicted prisoners and juvenile offenders with adult offenders. According to HRANA juvenile detainees were held alongside adult prisoners in some prisons, including specifically Saghez Central Prison in the province of Kurdistan. Authorities held women separately from men. According to the online media outlet, IranWire, infants under two years old are required to remain in prison with their mothers, and government statistics put the number of infant children currently in prison at 426. IranWire reported that multiple prisons across the country housed older children who lived with their incarcerated mothers without access to medical care or educational and recreational facilities.

Authorities often held political prisoners in separate prisons, wards, or in solitary confinement for long periods. Human rights activists and the international media also reported cases of political prisoners confined with accused and convicted violent criminals. Former prisoners reported that authorities often threatened political prisoners with transfer to criminal wards, where attacks were likely. HRANA reported that two political prisoners in Evin had been transferred to Ward Seven of the prison where they were attacked by nonpolitical prisoners on February 10.

There were reports of prisoner suicides. According to HRANA Mohsen Marzban committed suicide by ingesting pills on July 8 and died in Rajai Shahr Prison clinic. According to other prisoners, Marzban committed suicide because of continued harassment by the ward manager who routinely moved him to wards with violent prisoners where he was repeatedly attacked with knifes and other sharp objects.

Prison authorities often refused medical treatment for pre-existing conditions, injuries that prisoners suffered at the hands of prison authorities, and for illness due to the poor sanitary conditions in prison. According to ICHRI Kurdish women's activist Zeinab Jalalian, serving a life sentence for "enmity against God," was denied medical treatment or furlough despite the need for surgery for pterygium of the eye and boils on her tongue.

According to AI, Kurdish political prisoner, Afshin Sohrabzadeh, was denied medical care for intestinal cancer that resulted in recurring gastrointestinal bleeding. Originally arrested in Sanandaj in 2000 for membership in the banned Communist Party of Iran, he was sentenced to 25 years in prison and attempted suicide in 2013. He was granted brief medical leave on June 25 but was required to pay all his medical expenses in full, although he had coverage under Iran's national health care system. He has since been returned to detention.

The UN Working Group on Arbitrary Detention (WGAD) ruled Bahareh Hedayat's imprisonment since 2009 was arbitrary and against international law on June 14 and expressed "grave concern about Hedayat's deteriorating health since her detention in December 2009, particularly the allegations made by the source that she has not been provided with adequate medical care and that this may result in irreparable harm to her health and leave her permanently sterile." Hedayat, a women's and students' rights defender, was sentenced in 2010 to seven and a half years in prison for "interviews with foreign media," "insulting the supreme leader," "insulting the president," and "disrupting public order through participating in illegal gatherings." She was released on bail on September 3.

Omid Kokabee, a postdoctoral student imprisoned in 2011 and sentenced to 10 years for charges including "communicating with a hostile government," underwent kidney surgery in May where he remained chained to his hospital bed throughout treatment. Iranian media reported he had been granted conditional release by the Tehran Appeals Court on August 29.

According to IranWire, security officials routinely raided prison wards. During these raids guards beat both political and nonpolitical prisoners, performed nude body searches in front of other prisoners, and threatened prisoners' families. In some instances according to HRANA, guards singled out political prisoners for harsher treatment. On June 10, ICHRI published accounts of women prisoners reporting abusive behavior on the part of female prison guards aimed at humiliating them. This included verbal abuse, rough handling, and inappropriate and unnecessary physical contact.

Administration: Official public statistics on the prison population were limited. There were no reports on steps to improve recordkeeping or confirmation whether the penal system employed prison ombudspersons to respond to complaints. Authorities sometimes used alternatives to incarceration for nonviolent offenders, including probation, house arrest, employment bans, religious rehabilitation study, internal exile from their province of residence, and foreign travel bans.

Prisoners generally had access to visitors and telephone and other correspondence privileges weekly, but authorities often revoked these privileges. It was not known whether prisoners could practice religions other than Shia Islam while incarcerated. Prisoners were able to submit complaints to judicial authorities but often faced censorship and retribution for doing so (see section 1.a.). Authorities did not initiate credible investigations into allegations of inhuman conditions. Families of executed prisoners did not always receive notification of their deaths, and authorities frequently denied them the ability to perform funeral rights. HRANA reported that authorities of Uremia Central Prison refused to deliver the body of Kurdish political prisoner Mohammad Abdollahi to his family after his execution on August 8 and prohibited them from holding his funeral in a mosque.

Independent Monitoring: The government did not permit independent monitoring of prison conditions. Prisoners and their families often wrote letters to authorities and, in some cases, to UN bodies to highlight and protest their treatment. The UN Special Rapporteur reported that authorities sometimes subjected prisoners to threats after accusing them of contacting his office.

d. Arbitrary Arrest or Detention

Although the constitution prohibits arbitrary arrest and detention, they occurred frequently during the year. On December 19, authorities announced the publication of a Citizen's Rights Charter that enumerated various freedoms, including "security of their person, property, dignity, employment, legal and judicial process, social security, and the like." Its provisions were not implemented by year's end.

Role of the Police and Security Apparatus

Several agencies shared responsibility for law enforcement and maintaining order, including the Ministry of Intelligence and Security (MOIS) and law enforcement forces under the Interior Ministry, which report to the president, and the IRGC, which reports directly to the supreme leader. The Basij, a volunteer paramilitary group with local organizations across the country, sometimes acted as an auxiliary law enforcement unit subordinate to IRGC ground forces. Basij units often engaged in repression of political opposition elements or intimidation of civilians accused of violating the country's strict moral code without formal guidance or supervision from superiors. The supreme leader holds ultimate authority over all security agencies.

Corruption and impunity remained problems within police forces. Human rights groups frequently accused regular and paramilitary security forces, such as the Basij, of committing numerous human rights abuses, including acts of violence against protesters and participants in public demonstrations. According to July remarks from the Tehran Prosecutor General, Abbas Jafari-Dolatabadi, the attorney general is responsible for investigating and punishing security force abuses, but the process was not transparent, and there were few reports of government actions to discipline abusers.

Arrest Procedures and Treatment of Detainees

The constitution and penal code require a warrant or subpoena for an arrest and state that an arrested person should be informed of the charges against them within 24 hours. In a July meeting between the deputies of the General and Revolutionary Courts of Tehran, Tehran Prosecutor General, Jafari-Dolatabadi, stated, "regardless of the type of charge and positive evidences, the rights of the inmate must be taken into consideration in all respected cases, the judges should try to avoid infringement of the rights of the accused." Despite this statement, authorities often violated these procedures by holding some detainees, at times incommunicado, for weeks or months without charge or trial and frequently denying them contact with family or timely access to legal representation. The law obligates the government to provide indigent defendants with attorneys only for certain types of crimes. The courts set prohibitively high bail, even for lesser crimes and, in many cases, courts did not set bail. Authorities often compelled detainees and their families to submit property deeds to post bail, effectively silencing them due to fear of losing their families' property.

The government placed persons under house arrest without due process to restrict their movement and communication. At year's end former presidential candidates Mehdi Karroubi and Mir Hossein Mousavi, as well as Mousavi's wife Zahra Rahnavard, remained under house arrest imposed in 2011 without formal charges. Security forces restricted their access to visitors and limited their access to information.

Arbitrary Arrest: Authorities commonly used arbitrary arrests to impede alleged antiregime activities. Plainclothes officers arrived unannounced at homes or offices, arrested persons, conducted raids, and confiscated private documents, passports, computers, electronic media, and other personal items without warrants or assurances of due process. Individuals often remained in detention facilities for long periods without charges or trials, and authorities sometimes prevented them from informing others of their whereabouts for several days. Authorities often denied detainees' access to legal counsel during this period and imposed travel bans on individuals released on bail or pending trial.

Newspaper editor Sadra Mohaghegh was arrested on September 19 by security forces, which did not identify which security agency they represented or what he charges authorities placed against him. They raided his home and confiscated laptops and phones belonging to him and his family. He was released on bail on October 1.

Prominent political cartoonist Hadi Heidari, who was arrested without charges in November 2015, was released on parole in May.

Arbitrary and prolonged detentions of dual nationals--that is, individuals who are citizens of both Iran and another country--on politically motivated charges appeared to have increased during the year. Like other Iranians in similar situations, dual nationals generally faced a variety of due process violations, including lack of prompt access to a lawyer of their choosing, and brief trials during which they were not allowed access to evidence against them or the ability to defend them. In some cases courts sentenced such individuals to 10 years or more in prison.

<u>Detainee is Ability to Challenge Lawfulness of Detention before a Court</u>: Detainees are entitled to appeal their sentences in courts of law, but are not entitled to compensation for detention and were often held for extended periods without any legal proceedings.

<u>Pretrial Detention</u>: Pretrial detention was often arbitrarily lengthy, particularly in cases involving alleged violations of national security laws. According to Human Rights Watch (HRW), a judge may prolong detention at his discretion, and pretrial detention often lasted for months. Often authorities held pretrial detainees in custody with the general prison population.

<u>Amnesty</u>: According to the Constitution, the Supreme Leader may pardon or reduce the sentences of convicts upon a recommendation from the head of the judiciary. The supreme leader pardoned 705 prisoners on the holiday commemorating the birth of Imam Reza; none was a political prisoner, according to Fars News.

e. Denial of Fair Public Trial

The constitution provides that the judiciary be "an independent power" that is "free from every kind of unhealthy relation and connection." The court system was subject to political influence, and judges were appointed "in accordance with religious criteria." The supreme leader appoints the head of the judiciary. The head of the judiciary, members of the Supreme Court, and the prosecutor general were clerics. International observers continued to criticize the lack of independence of the country's judicial system and judges, and maintained that trials disregarded international standards of fairness.

Trial Procedures

According to the constitution and criminal procedure code, a defendant has the right to a fair trial, to be presumed innocent until convicted, to have access to a lawyer of his or her choice, and to appeal convictions in most cases that involve major penalties. These rights were not upheld. Panels of judges adjudicate trials in civil and criminal courts. Human rights activists reported trials in which authorities appeared to have determined the verdicts in advance, and defendants did not have the opportunity to confront their accusers, meet with lawyers, or have access to government-held evidence. The code of criminal procedure adopted in 2015 restricted the choice of attorneys to a government-approved list for defendants charged with crimes against national security and for journalists.

The government often charged political dissidents with vague crimes, such as "antirevolutionary behavior," "corruption on earth," "siding with global arrogance," "moharebeh," and "crimes against Islam." Prosecutors imposed strict penalties on government critics for minor violations. When post-revolutionary statutes did not address a situation, the government advised judges to give precedence to their knowledge and interpretation of "sharia" (Islamic law). Under this method judges may find a person guilty based on their own "divine knowledge," or they may issue more lenient sentences for persons who kill others considered "deserving of death." Authorities designed other trials, especially those of political prisoners, to publicize coerced confessions. On August 3, Tasnim News Agency aired video confessions of prisoners from Rajai Shahr Prison, some of whom were subsequently executed.

During the year human rights groups noted the absence of procedural safeguards in criminal trials. Courts admitted as evidence confessions made under duress or torture. In his March 10 report, the UN special rapporteur cited continuing "blindfolding, harassment, ill-treatment, torture, and coerced confessions during pretrial detention and interrogations." HRANA reported on March 7 that Tehran Chief of Police, Hossein Sajedinia, announced the arrest of more than a hundred "hooligans," who were jailed for a month without phone calls, visits, or access to a lawyer. Authorities allegedly beat the detainees until they recorded confessions admitting to crimes "disrupting social order."

The Special Clerical Court is headed by a Shia Islamic legal scholar, overseen by the supreme leader, and charged with investigating alleged offenses committed by clerics and issuing rulings based on an independent interpretation of Islamic legal sources. The constitution does not provide for the court, which operated outside the judiciary's purview. Clerical courts were used to prosecute Shia clerics who expressed controversial ideas and participated in activities outside the sphere of religion, such as journalism or reformist political activities.

Local media reported on the November 27 sentencing of prominent cleric, Hojjatoleslam Ahmad Montazeri, to 21 years in prison by the Qom branch of the Special Clerical Court for "endangering national security" and "leaking secrets of the Islamic system" after he posted audio recordings of his father, the late dissident cleric, Hossein Ali Montazeri, condemning the 1988 mass execution of political prisoners.

Political Prisoners and Detainees

Statistics regarding the number of citizens imprisoned for their political beliefs were not available. The human rights NGO United for Iran estimates there are 905 prisoners of conscience in Iran, including those jailed for their religious beliefs.

On May 18, the Guardian Council approved a new political crimes bill that defined political crimes and the treatment of political prisoners. The new law defines a political crime as an insult against the government, as well as "the publication of lies." It also includes any violation of a law governing political parties, trade associations, labor unions, Islamic organizations, election procedures, or religious minority groups. Such acts are defined as political crimes only if they "are committed with the intent of reforming the domestic or foreign policies of Iran" while those with the intent to damage "the foundations of the regime," are considered national security crimes. The court and the public prosecutor's office retain responsibility for determining the nature of the crime.

The new political crimes bill grants the accused certain rights during arrest and imprisonment. Political criminals are to be housed in jail facilities separate from ordinary criminals, exempted from wearing prison uniforms, not subject to the rules governing repeat offenses, not subject to extradition, and exempted from solitary confinement unless judicial officials deem it necessary. They also have the right to regularly see and correspond with immediate family and to access books, newspapers, radio, and television. The law came into effect in June; however, many of its provisions have not been implemented and the government continued to arrest and charge students, journalists, lawyers, political activists, women's activists, artists, and members of religious minorities and with "national security" crimes that did not fall under the political crimes bill.

The government reportedly held some persons in prison for years on unfounded charges of sympathizing with alleged terrorist groups. According to the press, NGOs, and the testimony of former prisoners, authorities often held political prisoners in solitary confinement for extended periods, denying them due process and access to legal representation. Political prisoners were also at greater risk of torture and abuse in detention and often mixed with the general prison population despite the political crimes bill stipulation that they have their own facilities. The government often placed political prisoners in prisons far from their families and denied them correspondence rights. The government issued travel bans on some former political prisoners, barred them from working in their professional sectors for years after incarceration, and imposed internal exile on others. The government did not permit international humanitarian organizations or UN representatives access to political prisoners.

Human rights defender and journalist, Narges Mohammadi, was sentenced to 16 years in prison by a revolutionary court in Tehran in May on charges of "propaganda against the state," "assembly and collusion against national security," and "establishing the antisecurity and illegal 'Step by Step to Stop the Death Penalty' party." An appeals court upheld her sentence on September 28. Prison authorities repeatedly denied her medical attention for pulmonary embolism and nerve system paralysis, as well as denying her family visitation and telephone calls, according to media reports.

During the year the government released some political prisoners, including dual Canadian-Iranian citizen, Homa Hoodfar, who was arrested in March on charges of fomenting a "feminist revolution" and released six months later. Authorities occasionally gave political prisoners suspended sentences and released them on bail with the understanding that renewed political activity could return them to prison. The government also tried to intimidate activists by temporarily suspending court proceedings against them, while leaving open the option of rearrest at any time. The government also summoned them repeatedly for questioning and confiscated personal belongings such as phones, laptops, and passports.

Lawyers who defended political prisoners were occasionally arrested. The government continued to imprison lawyers and others affiliated with the Defenders of Human Rights Center advocacy group. The health condition of human rights lawyer with the Center, Abdolfattah Soltani, deteriorated throughout the year. He was granted medical furlough on January 17 for 21 days, and returned to prison prior to full recovery, according to ICHRI. Originally imprisoned in 2011, he is serving a 13-year prison sentence for "being awarded the [2009] Nuremberg International Human Rights Award," "interviewing with the media about his clients' cases," and "co-founding the Defenders of Human Rights Center" with Nobel Peace laureate Shirin Ebadi.

The government has periodically jailed political activist and lawyer, Nasrin Sotoudeh, on various charges, and authorities briefly suspended her license to practice law due to her advocacy for prisoners of conscience. She was most recently summoned to appear in court on September 3 on unknown charges. According to ICHRI while her license to practice law has been reinstated, she is only allowed to take general civil cases and barred from working on any political or security related cases.

Civil Judicial Procedures and Remedies

Citizens had limited ability to sue the government and were not able to bring lawsuits against the government for civil or human rights violations through domestic courts.

Property Restitution

The constitution allows the government to confiscate property acquired illicitly or in a manner not in conformity with Islamic law. The government appeared to target ethnic and religious minorities in invoking this provision.

f. Arbitrary or Unlawful Interference with Privacy, Family, Home, or Correspondence

The constitution states that "reputation, life, property, [and] dwelling[s]" are protected from trespass, except as "provided by law." The government routinely infringed on this right. Security forces monitored the social activities of citizens, entered homes and offices, monitored telephone conversations and internet communications, and opened mail without court authorization.

Section 2. Respect for Civil Liberties, Including

a. Freedom of Speech and Press

The constitution provides for freedom of expression and of the press, except when words are deemed "detrimental to the fundamental principles of Islam or the rights of the public." According to the penal code, "anyone who engages in any type of propaganda against the Islamic Republic of Iran or in support of opposition groups and associations shall be sentenced to three months to one year of imprisonment." The law also provides for prosecution of persons accused of instigating crimes against the state or national security or "insulting" Islam. The government severely restricted freedom of speech and of the press and used the law to intimidate or prosecute persons who directly criticized the government or raised human rights problems, as well as to bring ordinary citizens into adherence with the government's moral code.

Freedom of Speech and Expression: Although the government issued a Citizen's Rights Charter with protections for free expression that states, "no one can be persecuted merely for his or her beliefs" on December 19, the law continues to limit freedom of speech, including by members of the press. Authorities did not permit individuals to criticize publicly the country's system of government, supreme leader, or official religion. Security forces and the country's judiciary punished those who violated these restrictions as well as those who publicly criticized the president, the cabinet, and the Islamic Consultative Assembly (parliament). The government monitored meetings, movements, and communications of its citizens and often charged persons with crimes against national security and insulting the regime based on letters, e-mails, and other public and private communications. Authorities threatened arrest or punishment for the expression of ideas or images they viewed as violations of the legal moral code.

According to AI retired university professor Mohammad Hossein Rafiee Fanood, who was in prison on charges of "spreading propaganda against the state," and "membership in an illegal group" was briefly hospitalized in August and returned to prison before full recovery. He was released on medical furlough in September, and has been banned from political and journalistic activities for two years.

Former President Mohamed Khatami remained barred from giving public remarks, and the media remained banned from publishing his name or image.

Press and Media Freedoms: The government's Press Supervisory Board issues press licenses, which it sometimes revoked in response to articles critical of the government or the regime, or did not renew for individuals facing criminal charges or incarcerated for political reasons. During the year the government banned, blocked, closed, or censored publications deemed critical of officials. The Ministry of Culture and Islamic Guidance ("Ershad") severely limited and controlled foreign media organizations' ability to work in the country by requiring foreign correspondents to provide detailed travel plans and topics of proposed stories before granting visas, limiting their ability to travel within the country, and forcing them to work with a local "minder."

Under the constitution private broadcasting is illegal. The government maintained a monopoly over all television and radio broadcasting facilities through the government agency, Islamic Republic of Iran Broadcasting (IRIB). Radio and television programming, the principal source of news for many citizens (especially in rural areas with limited internet access), reflected the government's political and socio-religious ideology. Independent print media companies existed, but the government severely limited their operations. There were reports of government "downlink" jamming of satellite broadcasts as signals entered the country. Satellite dishes remained illegal but ubiquitous. Those who distributed, used, or repaired satellite dishes faced fines up to 90 million rials ($2,800). Police launched campaigns to confiscate privately owned satellite dishes throughout the country under warrants provided by the judiciary. According to media reporting, Basij militia destroyed 100,000 confiscated satellite dishes on July 24.

Under the constitution the supreme leader appoints the head of the audiovisual policy agency; a council composed of representatives of the president, the judiciary, and parliament oversees the agency's activities. The Ministry of Culture reviews all potential publications, including foreign printed materials, prior to their domestic release, and may deem books unpublishable, remove text, or require word substitutions for terms deemed inappropriate.

Violence and Harassment: The government and its agents harassed, detained, abused, and prosecuted publishers, editors, and journalists, including those involved in internet-based media, for their reporting. The government also harassed many journalists' families. Reporters without Borders estimated that 19 journalists and 15 netizens remained in prison at year's end. International NGOs reported that authorities forced several citizen journalists into internal exile during the year.

Journalist Reyhaneh Tabatabaee began serving a one-year sentence on January 12 on charges of "propaganda against the regime" and was barred from using social media for two years. She was granted a four-day furlough on June 17.

There were updates in the cases of Issa Saharkhiz, Ehsan Mazandarani, Afarin Chitsaz, and Saman Safarzaie, arrested in 2015 on charges of membership in "an infiltration group connected to the United States and United Kingdom." Saharkhiz was sentenced to three years in prison on August 8 for "insulting the supreme leader" and "propagating against the state," and spent time in solitary confinement. According to the Committee to Protect Journalists (CPJ), the Prison Medical Examiner's Office ruled that Saharkhiz be released on medical grounds, but he remained in prison. According to reports on October 9, he has been on several hunger strikes. According to ICHRI Mazandarani was sentenced to 10 years' imprisonment, reduced to five years by the appeals court. He was temporarily released for medical treatment in October after suffering a heart attack while on hunger strike. Human Rights Watch reported that Chitsaz was sentenced to 10 years in prison on April 25 on charges of "assembly and collusion against national security," and "contact with foreign governments." The appeal court reduced her sentence to two years and a two-year ban from practicing journalism. She received a medical furlough for knee surgery in August. Safarzaie received a five-year imprisonment sentence in April for "assembly and collusion against national security." Tehran's appeals court reduced his sentence to two years in August, and according to ICHRI, as of November, he could be eligible for conditional release for lack of prior record and time already served in prison.

Cartoonist Atena Farghadani, imprisoned in 2014 for "spreading propaganda," "insulting members of parliament," and "insulting the supreme leader, was released on May 3 after an appeals court reduced her 12-year sentence to 18 months.

Censorship or Content Restrictions: The law forbids government censorship but also prohibits dissemination of information the government considers "damaging." During the year the government censored publications--both reformist and conservative--that criticized official actions or contradicted official views or versions of events. "Damaging" information included discussions of women's rights, the situation of minorities, criticism of government corruption, and references to mistreatment of detainees.

Officials routinely intimidated journalists into practicing self-censorship. Public officials often filed criminal complaints against newspapers, and the Press Supervisory Board, which regulates media content and publication, referred such complaints to the Press Court for further action, including closure, suspension, and fines. According to the IHRDC, the Islamic Republic News Agency (IRNA) determined the main topics and types of news to be covered and distributed topics required for reporting directly to various media outlets.

According to media reporting, the Press Supervisory Board temporarily revoked the publishing license of *Yalasarat al-Hosein* weekly paper in January for an article deemed insulting to the Vice President for Family and Women's Affairs, Shahindokht Mowlaverdi, and again in July for "offensive" comments about the spouses of prominent artists at an annual Television and Cinema awards ceremony in Tehran.

The Tehran Public and Revolutionary Prosecutor's office banned the daily *Qanun* newspaper on June 20 after the IRGC Intelligence Organization brought a case of "defamation" against *Qanun* for a June 11 article, "Damned 24 Hours," detailing the treatment of detainees in an unspecified Tehran prison. According to media reporting, the paper resumed publication on October 22 and was acquitted of the charges of "insulting religious sanctities" but found guilty of "publishing falsehoods."

Libel/Slander Laws: The government commonly used libel laws or cited national security to suppress criticism. According to the law, if any publication contains personal insults, libel, false statements, or criticism, the insulted individual has the right to respond in the publication within one month. According to the new crimes bill passed this year, "insult" or "libel" against the government, government representatives, or foreign officials while they are on Iranian soil, as well as "the publication of lies" with the intent to reform but not undermine the government are considered a political crimes and subject to certain trial and detention procedures (see section 1.e.). The government applied the law throughout the year, often citing statements made in various media outlets or internet platforms that criticized the government, to arrest, prosecute, and sentence individuals for crimes against national security.

Internet Freedom

Although Twitter is officially banned in the country, the government operated Twitter accounts under the names of Supreme Leader Khamenei, President Rouhani, Foreign Minister Zarif, and various other government-associated officials and entities.

The government restricted and disrupted access to the internet, monitored private online communications, and censored online content. Individuals and groups practiced self-censorship online. The Ministries of Culture, Information, and Communications Technology are the main regulatory bodies for content and internet systems in the country. The office of the supreme leader also houses a Supreme Council on Cyberspace charged with regulating content and systems. The government collected personally identifiable information in connection with citizens' peaceful expression of political, religious, or ideological opinion or beliefs.

According to the Ministry of Culture, 70 percent of Iranian youth between the ages of 15 and 29 used the internet. NGOs reported the government continued to filter content on the internet to ban access to particular sites and to filter traffic based on its content. The computer crimes law makes it illegal to distribute circumvention tools and virtual private networks, but the law is not clear whether the use of such tools is illegal, according to internet activists.

The ministry must approve all internet service providers. The government also requires all owners of websites and blogs in the country to register with the agencies that comprise the Committee in Charge of Determining Unauthorized Websites, the governmental organization that determines censoring criteria. These include the Ministry of Culture, the Ministry of Information and Communications Technology, the MOIS, and the Tehran Public Prosecutor's Office.

Local media reported on the launch of Iran's "National Information Network," on August 14 to provide a "faster, more secure" service. Internet activists reported many individuals were unable to access Facebook and several other social media outlets, even when using various circumvention tools, after the program was launched. RWB reported that this National Information Network is intended to act like an "intranet," system, with full content control and user identification. Authorities can disconnect this network from World Wide Web content and reportedly will use it to provide government propaganda while blocking access to independently reported news or freely gathered information.

The same law that applies to traditional media applies to electronic media, and the Press Supervisory Board and judiciary invoked the law to close websites during the year. Six media outlets--*Borna*, *Mawj*, *Bahar*, *Puyesh*, *Persian Khodro*, *9 Sobh*, and *Memari*--were blocked and/or reprimanded in September for reporting on corruption scandals in several Tehran property developments. They received official reprimands for violating the cybercrimes law, according to local media reports.

Authorities continue to block online messaging tools such as Facebook and Twitter. The IRGC Center for Combating Organized Crime website reported on August 23 that IRGC forces had summoned, detained, and warned some 450 administrators of social media groups over "immoral" content.

An estimated 20 million Iranians use the online messaging application Telegram, which has security features that make the content of users' communications more difficult to be read by a third party. CPJ nevertheless reported in June that users were at risk of being monitored, as had happened with other similar applications in the past. Iran's Supreme Council of Cyberspace announced on May 29 that Telegram had one year to move all of its data to servers inside Iran or risk being closed entirely. Telegram users in Iran continued to be harassed for content posted through its servers. According to local media reports, the Iranian Cyber Police arrested three Telegram channels administrators on August 9 for publishing material "insulting religious sanctities."

Government organizations, including the Basij "Cyber Council," the Cyber Police, and the Cyber Army, which observers presumed to be controlled by the IRGC, monitored, identified, and countered alleged cyber threats to national security. These organizations especially targeted citizens' activities on social networking websites officially banned by the Committee in Charge of Determining Offensive Content, such as Facebook, Twitter, YouTube, and Flickr, and reportedly harassed persons who criticized the government or raised sensitive social problems. Radio Zamaneh reported on April 21 that hackers who may have been associated with governmental security offices hacked Vice President Shahindokht Mowlaverdi's private e-mail account and sent spearfishing e-mails to her contacts.

International media reported that Iranian national soccer team player, Sosha Makani, was suspended from the league in June for "inappropriate conduct" after photos emerged online of him wearing yellow "SpongeBob" pants.

Eight online models were arrested, and an unannounced number of online Instagram, Telegram, and Facebook pages were closed in May for "immoral content" after images were posted that did not adhere to government-sanctioned dress requirements. The Tehran Prosecutor General announced the arrests were part of operations "Spider I" and "Spider II," which sought to identify illicit modeling activity online.

Ministry of Information and Communications Technology regulations prohibit households and cybercafes from having high-speed internet access. The government periodically reduced internet speed to discourage downloading material; however, in general there were slight improvements to speed as the government expanded access to 3G services for mobile devices.

According to the UN special rapporteur's reports, serious difficulties persisted, including severe content restrictions, intimidation and prosecution of users, and limitations on access through the intentional slowing of service and filtering. The most heavily blocked websites were in the arts, society, politics, and news categories. RWB reported there were more than 800 cases of censorship since the start of the year.

Academic Freedom and Cultural Events

The government significantly restricted academic freedom and the independence of higher education institutions. Authorities systematically targeted university campuses to suppress social and political activism by prohibiting independent student organizations, imprisoning student activists, removing faculty, preventing students from enrolling or continuing their education because of their political or religious affiliation or activism, and restricting social sciences and humanities curricula.

Authorities barred Baha'i students from higher education and harassed those who pursued education through the unrecognized online university of the Baha'i Institute for Higher Education (BIHE) (see International Religious Freedom Report).

The government maintained controls on cinema, music, theater, and art exhibits, and censored those deemed to transgress Islamic values. The government censored or banned films deemed to promote secularism, non-Islamic ideas about women's rights, unethical behavior, drug abuse, violence, or alcoholism. According to the IHRDC, the nine-member film review council of the Ministry of Culture made up of clerics, former directors, former parliamentarians, and academics, must approve the content of every film before production and again before screening. Films can also be arbitrarily barred from the screen even if all the appropriate permits were received in advance.

According to the IHRDC, Minister of Culture and Islamic Guidance Ali Jannati pulled the film *Fifty Kilos of Sour Cherries* from theaters after its initial screening in Tehran, for promoting the "disintegration and demise of the family and providing an inappropriate example through the actress's makeup."

The ministry's Film Evaluation and Supervision Department banned five filmmakers--Mostafa Kiyai, Alireza Sartipi, Abdollah Alikhani, Sayyed Amir Parvin-Hoseini, and Reza Mirkarmi--and three film companies--Filmiran, Nur-e Taban, and Puya Film--in August from receiving permits or services in response to allegations they had advertised on foreign-based Persian-language satellite TV channels and "hostile networks run by the enemies of the Islamic Republic."

Filmmaker Kayvan Karimi, initially sentenced in 2015 to six years in prison for "insulting the sanctities" in his documentary film on political graffiti, had his sentence reduced to one year by an appeals court in February. He was also sentenced to 223 lashes for "having illegitimate relations" with a woman who is not a relative." Authorities originally arrested Karimi on these charges in 2013. He began serving his sentence on November 23.

According to international media reports, authorities released filmmaker Mostafa Azizi in April; he had been sentenced in June 2015 to eight years in prison for "propaganda against the state," "acting against national security in cyberspace," and "insulting the supreme leader."

Officials continued to discourage teaching music in schools. Authorities considered heavy metal and foreign music religiously offensive, and police continued to repress underground concerts and arrest musicians and music distributors. The Ministry of Culture must officially approve a song's lyrics, music, and album covers as complying with the country's moral values, although many underground musicians released albums without seeking such permission.

Mehdi Rajabian, Hossein Rajabian, and Yousef Emadi, originally arrested in 2013, were found guilty of "insulting Islamic sanctities," "spreading propaganda against the system," and "illegal audio-visual activities" in May for the distribution of unlicensed music. They were sentenced to three years' detention and fined 200 million rials ($6,178). Authorities shut down their website, and AI reported the three were allegedly beaten and given electric shocks while in detention. According to ICHRI the two Rajabian brothers started hunger strikes on September 8 to protest their separation in different wards and lack of access to medical care for Mehdi Rajabian for symptoms of multiple sclerosis.

Rapper Amir "Tataloo" Hossein Maghsoodloo, was detained by police on August 23 in Tehran for "spreading depravity among youth."

Authorities in several provinces cancelled concerts they deemed "inappropriate" throughout the year. Local authorities cancelled the concerts of singer Salar Aghili and musicians Shahram Nazeri and Kayvan Kalhor, despite having received the necessary prior permits from the Ministry of Culture. Prosecutor Gholamali Sadeghi of Khorasan Razavi Province announced in August that no more music concerts would be allowed to take place in the province.

b. Freedom of Peaceful Assembly and Association

Freedom of Assembly

The constitution permits assemblies and marches of unarmed persons "provided they do not violate the principles of Islam." The government restricted this right and closely monitored gatherings such as public entertainment and lectures, student and women's meetings and protests, meetings and worship services of minority religious groups, labor protests, online gatherings and networking, funeral processions, and Friday prayer gatherings to prevent anything it considered as antiregime. According to activists the government arbitrarily applied rules governing permits to assemble, with pro-regime groups rarely experiencing difficulty and groups viewed as critical of the regime experiencing harassment regardless of whether authorities issued a permit.

Iranian Students News Agency (ISNA) reported on the October 30 arrest of organizers of a gathering celebrating the birth of Achaemenid King Cyrus the Great on October 28 in Fars province for "norm breaking and antivalues" slogans. ICHRI reported more than 70 individuals held since October were sentenced in December to serve between three months to eight years for participating in and organizing the event.

According to a report by ICHRI on December 2, security agents arrested Nasser Zarafshan, prominent human rights lawyer and several members of the Writers'

Association of Iran at a commemoration event for victims of the "chain murders" of dissidents in the 1990s.

Freedom of Association

The constitution provides for the establishment of political parties, professional and political associations, and Islamic and recognized religious minority organizations, as long as such groups do not violate the principles of freedom, sovereignty, national unity, or Islamic criteria; or question Islam as the basis of the country's system of government. The government limited freedom of association through threats, intimidation, the imposition of arbitrary requirements on organizations, and the arrests of group leaders and members.

Teachers were barred from commemorating International Labor Day and Teachers' Day, and several teachers' union activists remained in prison, including Mahmoud Beheshti Langroudi, Esmail Abdi, Mohammad Davari, Mohammad Reza Niknejad, Mehdi Bohlooli, and Mahmoud Bagheri. Esmail Abdi, the general secretary of the Iranian Teachers' Trade Association, was charged with "propaganda against the Islamic system" and "conspiracy to disrupt the security of the country." Mahmoud Beheshti Langroudi, spokesperson of the Iranian Teachers' Trade Association, was sentenced to six years in prison on charges of "colluding against national security" and "propaganda against the state." Both Langroudi and Abdi, who reportedly did not have access to a lawyer, engaged in hunger strikes to protest prison conditions. Langroudi was released on a temporary medical furlough on May 11 after complications arose from his strike, according to ICHRI. Abdi was also released on bail. Both were ordered back to prison in October after a Tehran Appeals Court upheld their six-year prison sentences.

c. Freedom of Religion

See the Department of State's *International Religious Freedom Report* at www.state.gov/religiousfreedomreport/.

d. Freedom of Movement, Internally Displaced Persons, Protection of Refugees, and Stateless Persons

The constitution provides for freedom of internal movement, foreign travel, emigration, and repatriation, but the government restricted these rights. The government cooperated with the Office of the UN High Commissioner for Refugees (UNHCR) with regard to refugees from Afghanistan and Iraq.

<u>In-country Movement</u>: Judicial sentences sometimes included internal exile after release from prison, which prevented individuals from traveling to certain provinces. Women often required the supervision of a male guardian or chaperone to travel and faced official and societal harassment for traveling alone. Refugees faced restrictions on in-country movement and faced restrictions or bars from entering 28 provinces according to UNHCR.

<u>Foreign Travel</u>: The government required exit permits for foreign travel for all citizens. Citizens who were educated at government expense or received scholarships had to either repay the scholarship or receive a temporary permit to exit the country. The government restricted the foreign travel of some religious leaders, members of religious minorities, and scientists in sensitive fields. Several journalists, academics, opposition politicians, human and women's rights activists, and artists remained subject to foreign travel bans and had their passports confiscated during the year. Married women were not allowed to travel outside the country without prior permission from their husbands.

<u>Exile</u>: The law does not provide for forced exile abroad. Many citizens practiced self-imposed exile to express their beliefs freely or escape government harassment.

Protection of Refugees

The government had a mixed record in providing support for refugees, mostly from Afghanistan and some from Iraq. The government is responsible for refugee registration and status determination and has granted registration to 960,000 Afghan and 28,000 Iraqi refugees under a system known as "Amayesh," through which authorities provide refugees with cards identifying them as legally registered refugees. The cards enable refugees to access basic services, and facilitate the issuance of work permits to refugees. Additionally, approximately 1.4 million "non-refugee" Afghans held visas under a Joint Action Plan for formerly undocumented Afghans. A large number of undocumented Afghans lived in the country and were unable to register as official refugees or visa holders. During a visit to Tehran in April, UNHCR Assistant High Commissioner George Okoth-Obbo stated the number of unregistered Afghans was about three million.

Supreme Leader Khamenei stated on November 22 "Iran has for years hosted three million Afghans, and has provided them with the conditions to study and live in Iran, and has, with complete tolerance, adopted a humane attitude towards migrants." The HRW reported that the government continued its mistreatment of

Afghans in the country, including deportations, physical abuse by security forces, and restricted access to education or jobs.

Access to Asylum: The law provides for the granting of asylum or refugee status to qualified applicants. While the government reportedly has a system for providing protection to refugees, UNHCR did not have information regarding how the country made asylum determinations. According to HRW the government continued to block many Afghans from registering to obtain refugee status. Afghans not currently registered under the Amayesh system that had migrated to Iran in the past decades of conflict in their home country continued to be denied asylum or access to register with the United Nations as refugees for resettlement. NGOs reported many of these displaced asylum seekers felt pressured to leave the country but could not return to Afghanistan because of the security situation in their home provinces.

Refoulement: According to activist groups and NGOs, authorities routinely arrested Afghan refugees and sometimes threatened them with refoulement. According to a HRW report, government military recruiters threatened unregistered Afghan refugees with deportation or barred them from registering as refugees if they did not join military forces when asked to do so.

Employment: Only refugees with government-issued work permits as part of the Amayesh system were able to work. NGO sources reported that cards were difficult to renew and were often prohibitively expensive for refugees to maintain due to steep annual renewal fees.

Access to Basic Services: Amayesh cardholders have access to primary education and received primary health care, including vaccinations, prenatal care, maternal and child health, and family planning from the Ministry of Health. Under a 2015 agreement, they also had access to the Salamat Insurance Program and benefit from a health insurance package for hospitalization similar to Iranian nationals, and those with qualifying "special diseases" got comprehensive coverage. The supreme leader announced in 2015 that all Afghans, regardless of status, should have access to school. According to UNHCR's website, more than 350,000 Afghan and Iraqi students (both registered and unregistered) were enrolled in the 2015-2016 academic year. According to media reporting on schools for Afghan children, however, Afghans continued to have difficulty gaining access to education. The government also sometimes imposed fees for children of registered refugees to attend public schools or required unregistered children to have legal immigration status.

There were barriers to marriage between citizens and displaced Afghans. Authorities require Afghans to obtain documentation from their embassy or government offices in Afghanistan to register their marriage in the country, according to media reporting. The Family Protection Law states, "any foreigner who marries an Iranian woman without the permission of the Iranian government will be sentenced to two to five years in prison plus a cash penalty." Furthermore, authorities only considered the children born from such unions eligible for citizenship if the child's father is a citizen and registers the child as his, leaving many children stateless.

Most provinces' residency limitations on refugees effectively denied them access to public services, such as public housing, in the restricted areas of those provinces.

Stateless Persons

Due to documentation restraints, there are no accurate numbers on how many stateless persons reside in the country. Stateless persons include those without birth documents or refugee identification cards. They are subjected to inconsistent government policies and rely on charities, principally domestic, to provide medical care and schooling. Authorities prohibited stateless persons from receiving formal government support or travel documents.

Women may not directly transmit citizenship to their children or to noncitizen spouses. Under a 2006 amendment to the Nationality Law, only children born to Iranian mothers and non-Iranian fathers who reside in Iran for 18 years and whose parent's marriage is officially registered with the government are eligible to apply for citizenship. According to media reports, between 400,000 and one million persons lacked Iranian nationality despite having an Iranian citizen mother due to limitations on citizenship transmission.

Section 3. Freedom to Participate in the Political Process

The constitution provides citizens the ability to choose the president, as well as members of the Assembly of Experts and Islamic Consultative Assembly (parliament), peacefully through elections based on universal suffrage, but candidate vetting conducted by unelected bodies abridged this right in all instances. The Assembly of Experts, which is composed of 86 popularly elected clerics who serve eight-year terms, elects the supreme leader, who acts as the recognized head of state and may be removed only by a vote of the assembly. The Guardian Council vets and qualifies candidates for all Assembly of Experts, presidential, and parliamentary elections based on criteria that include candidates' allegiance to the state and Shia Islam. The council consists of six clerics appointed by the supreme leader and six jurists nominated by the head of the judiciary and approved by parliament. There is no separation of state and religion, and certain clerics had significant influence in the government.

Elections and Political Participation

<u>Recent Elections</u>: The country's electoral system continued to fall short of international standards for free, fair elections because of the Guardian Council's preeminent roles in the political process, including determining which individuals could run for office, and removing elected candidates. In February both Assembly of Experts and Islamic Consultative Assembly, elections were held. Prior to the elections, the Guardian Council disqualified 79 percent of the candidates running for the Assembly of Experts (including all female candidates) and 58 percent running for the Islamic Consultative Assembly, with media reporting only 1 percent of registered reformist candidates were allowed to run. Voter turnout for the election was around 62 percent, and runoff elections for those seats where no candidate won an outright majority were held in May. Minoo Khalegi from Isfahan District had her election to the Islamic Consultative Assembly nullified by the Guardian Council after she was deemed "unfit" to hold office. Outside observers were not permitted to monitor the elections, but media reporting indicated that there was no apparent vote tampering.

In 2013 voters elected Hassan Rouhani president. The Interior Ministry announced that Rouhani won 50.88 percent of the votes with a 72 percent turnout of eligible voters. The Guardian Council approved eight candidates for president from 686 individuals who registered as candidates. It did not approve any female registrants. The UN special rapporteur reported that several candidates were excluded because of involvement in postelection protests in 2009.

<u>Political Parties and Political Participation</u>: The constitution provides for the formation of political parties, but the Interior Ministry granted licenses only to parties in adherence with the "velayat-e faqih" system of government embodied in the constitution. Registered political organizations that adhered to the system generally operated without restriction, but most were small, focused around an individual, and without nationwide membership. Members of political parties and

persons with any political affiliation that the regime deemed unacceptable faced harassment, violence, and sometimes imprisonment.

The government maintained bans on several opposition organizations and political parties. Security officials continued to harass, intimidate, and arrest members of the political opposition and some reformists (see section 1.e.). Kourosh Zaim, a leading party activist of the banned National Front Party, was arrested on July 16 and sentenced to four years in prison based on a 2015 suspended sentence for "propaganda against the State." This was his fourth arrest based on his political activity, according to ICHRI.

<u>Participation of Women and Minorities</u>: Women faced significant legal, religious, and cultural barriers to political participation. According to the Guardian Council's interpretation, the constitution bars women and persons of foreign origin from serving as supreme leader or president, as members of the Assembly of Experts, the Guardian Council, or the Expediency Council, as well as certain types of judges. In 2013 the Guardian Council disqualified all 30 women who registered as presidential candidates. Eighteen women won seats in the 290-member parliament in February's election, and 17 were sworn in in May. Women served in senior government positions, including the Vice President for Legal Affairs, the Minister of Environmental Protection, and the Vice President of Women and Family Affairs.

Practitioners of religions other than Shia Islam are barred from serving as supreme leader or president and from membership in the Assembly of Experts, the Guardian Council, or the Expediency Council. The law reserves five seats in parliament for members of recognized minority religious groups, although minorities can also be elected to nonreserved seats. The five reserved seats were filled by one Zoroastrians, one Jew, and three Christians. There were no non-Muslims in the cabinet or on the Supreme Court.

Section 4. Corruption and Lack of Transparency in Government

The law provides criminal penalties for official corruption, but the government did not implement the law effectively, and corruption was a serious and ubiquitous problem. Officials in all branches of government frequently engaged in corrupt practices with impunity. Many officials expected bribes for providing routine services or received bonuses outside their regular work. Individuals routinely bribed officials to obtain permits for illegal construction.

Endowed religious charitable foundations, or "bonyads," accounted for a quarter to a third of the country's economy according to some experts. Government insiders, including members of the military and clergy, ran these tax-exempt organizations, which are defined under law as charities. Members of the political opposition and international corruption watchdog organizations frequently accused bonyads of corruption. Bonyads received benefits from the government, but no government agency must publicly approve their budgets.

Numerous companies and subsidiaries affiliated with the IRGC engaged in trade and business activities, sometimes illicitly, in the telecommunications, mining, and construction sectors. Other IRGC entities reportedly engaged in smuggling pharmaceutical products, narcotics, and raw materials. The domestic and international press similarly reported that individuals with strong government connections had access to foreign currency at preferential exchange rates, allowing them to exploit a gap between the country's black market and official exchange rates.

According to media reports, businessman Babak Zanjani, originally arrested in 2013 on corruption charges, was sentenced to death in March for "corruption on earth." Iran's Supreme Court confirmed his death sentence on December 4. His sentence had not been carried out at year's end.

Local media reported on October 31 that a special court for civil servants had reached a verdict against former Social Security Organization (SSO) Head Saeed Mortazavi for alleged financial wrongdoings. Charges against Mortazavi include selling stakes in 137 SSO-owned companies at a below-market price of more than 32 trillion rials (four billion dollars) to a holding company owned by jailed billionaire Babak Zanjani; giving gift cards to dozens of government officials and members of parliament; and paying 1.5 billion rials ($60,000) to state television to cover the SSO's 60th anniversary celebrations.

Numerous government agencies existed to fight corruption, including the Anticorruption Headquarters, the Anticorruption Task Force, the Committee to Fight Economic Corruption, and the General Inspection Organization. Parliament's Article 90 Commission also had authority to investigate complaints of corruption within the government. Information was unavailable regarding these organizations' specific mandates, their collaboration with civil society, and whether they operated effectively, independently, and with sufficient resources.

<u>Financial Disclosure</u>: Regulations require government officials, including cabinet ministers and members of the Guardian Council, the Expediency Council, and the Assembly of Experts, to submit annual financial statements to the government inspectorate. Little information was available on whether the government effectively implemented the law, whether officials obeyed the law, or whether financial statements were publicly accessible. Government officials capped salaries for public employees and politicians after leaked salary pay slips of government officials exposed high salaries and unregistered bonuses, according to local media.

<u>Public Access to Information</u>: While parliament has a centralized website with the docket of pending legislation, lists of committee representation, and voting patterns, the law does not mandate public access to government information. Some government agencies maintain websites documenting their activities, but they published only those documents they selected, and there is no public mechanism for forcing open records of activity for public review.

Fars News Agency reported on October 26 that journalist, Yashar Soltani, was arrested in September and charged with "publishing a confidential report" by Tehran's Revolutionary and Public Prosecutor's office. His news website published a State Inspectorate Organization report that contained a list of officials, mostly Tehran Council members and senior municipal managers, who allegedly bought properties in Tehran's prestigious districts at "a remarkable discount." He remained in prison at year's end and has been denied bail.

Section 5. Governmental Attitude Regarding International and Nongovernmental Investigation of Alleged Violations of Human Rights

The government restricted the work of human rights groups and activists and often responded to their inquiries and reports with harassment, arrests, online hacking, and monitoring of individual activists and organization workplaces.

The government restricted the operations of and did not cooperate with local or international human rights NGOs investigating alleged violations of human rights. Legally, NGOs must register with the Ministry of Interior and apply for permission to receive foreign grants. Independent human rights groups and other NGOs faced continued harassment because of their activism, as well as the threat of closure by government officials following prolonged and often arbitrary delays in obtaining official registration.

During the year the government prevented some human rights defenders, civil society activists, journalists, and scholars from traveling abroad. Human rights activists reported intimidating telephone calls, threats of blackmail, online hacking attempts, and property damage from unidentified law enforcement and government officials. Government officials sometimes harassed and arrested family members of human rights activists. Courts routinely suspended sentences of human rights activists, leaving open the option for authorities to arrest or imprison individuals arbitrarily at any time on the previous charges.

In his March report, the UN Special Rapporteur on the Situation of Human Rights in Iran expressed concern at the arrest, arbitrary detention, and sentencing of human rights defenders, student activists, journalists, and lawyers. He noted acts of intimidation and reprisals in detention, including torture and mistreatment. He also expressed concern over reports of reprisals against human rights defenders for engagement with the UN Special Rapporteur and for cooperation with other UN mechanisms.

The government continued to deny requests from international human rights NGOs to establish offices in or to conduct regular investigative visits to the country. The most recent visit of international human rights NGO was by AI in 2004 as part of the European Union's human rights dialogue with the country.

<u>The United Nations or Other International Bodies</u>: During the year the government ignored or denied repeated requests for visits from UN special rapporteurs. It participated in the current year's Geneva-based UN Human Rights Council's quadrennial universal periodic review of its human rights record, met with the Special Rapporteur in Geneva in 2015, and participated in the Committee on the Rights of the Child periodic review in January. According to NGO sources, including HRW and AI, the government's rights record and its level of cooperation with international rights institutions remained poor. The most recent visit by a UN human rights agency was in 2005.

During the year the UN Human Rights Commission renewed the resolution establishing the mandate for a human rights rapporteur for the country and appointed Asma Jahangir as the new special rapporteur in September. The previous special rapporteur, Ahmed Shaheed, officially commenced work in 2011, but the government denied his repeated requests to visit the country.

On November 15, for the 14th consecutive year, the UN General Assembly adopted a resolution expressing deep concern about the country's "serious ongoing and recurring human rights violations." The resolution also noted the government's lack of cooperation with UN mechanisms, including its poor implementation of the recommendations it accepted during the universal periodic review and its continued failure to allow the UN special rapporteur into the country to investigate human rights abuses. The resolution also cited the government's failure to approve any request from a UN thematic special procedures mandate holder to visit the country in over a decade.

Government Human Rights Bodies: The High Council for Human Rights, headed by Mohammad Javad Larijani, is part of the judicial branch of the government and lacks independence. The council continued to defend the imprisonment of high-profile human rights defenders and political opposition leaders, despite domestic and international pressure. Larijani continued to call for an end of the position of UN special rapporteur. There was no information available whether the council challenged any laws or court rulings during the year.

Section 6. Discrimination, Societal Abuses, and Trafficking in Persons

Women

Rape and Domestic Violence: Rape is illegal and subject to strict penalties, including death, but it remained a problem. The law considers sex within marriage consensual by definition and, therefore, does not address spousal rape, including in cases of forced marriage.

Cases of rape were difficult to document due to nonreporting. Most rape victims likely did not report the crime because they feared retaliation or punishment for having been raped, including charges of indecency, immoral behavior, or adultery, the last of which carries the death penalty. They also feared societal reprisal or ostracism. For a conviction of rape, the law requires four Muslim men or a combination of three men and two women, two men and four women, to have witnessed a rape. A woman or man found making a false accusation of rape is subject to 80 lashes.

The law does not prohibit domestic violence. The Census Bureau, the government agency responsible for data collection, does not permit international organizations to study domestic violence in the country. Authorities consider abuse in the family a private matter and seldom discussed it publicly.

<u>Female Genital Mutilation/Cutting (FGM/C)</u>: The penal code criminalizes FGM/C and states "the cutting or removing of the two sides of female genitalia leads to "diyeh" (financial penalty or blood money) equal to half the full amount of "diyeh" for the woman's life." Whether there were prosecutions for FGM/C during the year is unknown. The UN Committee on the Rights of the Child noted in its January periodic review that despite the criminalization of FGM/C, it continued to occur with impunity, especially in the provinces of Kurdistan, Western Azerbaijan, Kermanshah, Ilam, Lorestan, and Hormozgan. When the mutilation occurred, it was usually performed on girls under the age of 10. A March study on Kermanshah Province suggested that FGM/C was a common practice among women there, with more than 58 percent of girls circumcised; traditional midwives performed 98 percent of the mutilations at the mother's request.

<u>Other Harmful Traditional Practices</u>: There were no official reports of killings motivated by "honor" or other harmful traditional practices during the year, although human rights activists reported that such killings continued to occur, particularly among rural and tribal populations. The penal code reduces punitive measures for fathers and other family members who murder or physically harm children in domestic violence or "honor killings." Under the law the principal of "qisas" (punishment in kind) does not apply to murders within the family committed by the father. If a man is found guilty of murdering his daughter, the punishment is between three and 10 years in prison rather than the normal death sentence or payment of "diyeh" for homicide cases.

<u>Sexual Harassment</u>: The law addresses sexual harassment in the context of physical contact between men and women and prohibits physical contact between unrelated men and women. There was no reliable data on the extent of sexual harassment, but women and human rights observers reported that sexual harassment was the norm in many workplaces. There were no known government efforts to combat and address this issue. The country's state-run English language television channel, Press TV, suspended two executives in February after reports emerged they had been sexually harassing female staff.

<u>Reproductive Rights</u>: The law recognizes the basic right of married couples to decide freely and responsibly the number, spacing, and timing of their children. Couples are entitled to reproductive healthcare, free from discrimination, coercion, and violence. While government healthcare previously included full free access to contraception and family planning for married couples, state family planning cuts in 2012 reducing the budget to almost zero remained in place.

<u>Discrimination</u>: The constitution provides for equal protection for women under the law in conformity with its interpretation of Islam. The government did not enforce the law, however, and provisions in the Islamic civil and penal codes, particularly sections dealing with family and property law, discriminate against women and restricted women's economic, social, political, academic, and cultural rights.

Women may not transmit citizenship to their children or to a noncitizen spouse. The government does not recognize marriages between Muslim women and non-Muslim men, irrespective of their citizenship. The law states that a virgin woman or girl wishing to wed needs the consent of her father or grandfather or the court's permission, even if she is over the age of 18.

The law permits a man to have as many as four wives and an unlimited number of "sigheh" (temporary wives), based on a Shia custom under which couples can enter into a limited time civil and religious contract, which outlines the union's conditions. The law does not grant temporary wives and any resulting children rights associated with traditional marriage, but the contract is enforceable, and recognized children can obtain documentation and have limited rights.

A woman has the right to divorce if her husband signs a contract granting that right, cannot provide for his family, has violated the terms of their original marriage contract, or is a drug addict, insane, or impotent. A husband is not required to cite a reason for divorcing his wife. Traditional interpretations of Islamic law recognize a divorced woman's right to part of shared property and to alimony. These laws were not always enforced, and the ability of a woman to seek divorce was limited. According to ISNA if a personal maintenance allowance is not paid, the wife may "reject all legal and religious obligations" to her husband. By law such an allowance may be requested during the marriage as well as after a divorce, and if it is not paid, the woman may sue her former husband in court.

The civil code provides divorced women preference in custody for children up to age seven, but fathers maintain legal guardianship rights over the child and must agree on many legal aspects of the child's life (such as issuing travel documents, enrolling in school, or the filing of a police report). After the child reaches the age of seven, the father is granted custody unless he is proven unfit to care for the child. Courts determine custody in disputed cases. Once children reach the legal age of maturity, the court must also consider the preference of the child in determining the custody arrangement.

Women sometimes received disproportionate punishment for crimes such as adultery, including death sentences (see section 1.a.). The Islamic penal code retains provisions that value a woman's testimony in a court of law as half that of a man's, and a woman's life as half that of a man's. According to the penal code, the "diyeh" (blood money) paid in the death of a woman is half the amount of a death of a man, with the exception of car accident insurance payments.

According to 2012 UN statistics, the female youth literacy rate was 98.5 percent, and the adult female literacy rate was 90.3 percent. Women had access to primary and advanced education, although the percentage of female students entering universities decreased from 62 percent in 2007-2008 to 42 percent in the current year as a result gender-rationing policies implemented in 2012. Quotas and other restrictions, which varied across universities, limited women's undergraduate admissions to certain fields, as well as to certain master's and doctoral programs.

Social and legal constraints limited women's professional opportunities, and the unemployment rate for women was nearly twice that for men. Women were represented in many fields, including in government and police forces but the law requires a married woman to obtain her husband's permission to work. The law does not provide that women and men must be paid equally for equal work. According to a 2015 survey for the World Economic Forum's *Global Gender Gap Report*, women earned on average 58 percent as much money as their male counterparts for similar work. Women may not serve in many high-level political positions or as judges, except as consultants or research judges without the power to impose sentences.

Women faced discrimination in home and property ownership, as well as access to financing. In cases of inheritance, male heirs receive twice the inheritance of their female counterparts. The government enforced gender segregation in many public spaces, including for patients during medical care, and prohibited women from mixing openly with unmarried men or men not related to them. In 2015 the deputy minister for sports announced women would be permitted to enter sports stadiums and attend some sporting events, but authorities did not implement the new policy. Women must ride in a reserved section on public buses and enter some public buildings, universities, and airports through separate entrances. While riding a bicycle is not legally a crime for women in Iran, religious and local authorities in Marivan, Kurdistan banned women from riding bicycles in public. International media reported that several women were arrested and forced to sign pledges that they would cease riding bicycles after being stopped by authorities on July 26.

The law provides that a woman who appears in public without appropriate attire, such as a cloth scarf veil ("hejab") over the head and a long jacket ("manteau"), or a large full-length cloth covering ("chador"), may be sentenced to flogging and fined. Absent a clear legal definition of "appropriate covering" or of the punishment, women were subjected to the opinions of disciplinary forces, police, security forces, or judges. In September local media reported that police barred 800 shops from selling women's clothing with controversial slogans like "I am queen" and "no rules." Iranian media reported on the announcement of the expansion of Tehran's morality police force to include 7,000 additional undercover agents to police "bad hejab."

Children

The country established the National Body on the Convention on the Rights of the Child in 2012 to promote the Convention on the Rights of the Child, to which Iran is signatory. The body, which reviews draft regulations and legislation relating to child rights, is not independent and is overseen by the Ministry of Justice. The country underwent a periodic panel review by the UN Committee on the Rights of the Child in January. The review noted many concerns, including discrimination against girls; children with disabilities; unregistered, refugee, and migrant children; and LGBTI children. The 2015 updates to the penal code called for the establishment of a separate juvenile court system, and male juvenile detainees were held in separate Rehabilitation Centers in most urban areas. Nevertheless, female juvenile detainees and male juvenile detainees in rural areas were held alongside adults in detention facilities, according to NGO reports presented to the UN Committee on the Rights of the Child.

Birth Registration: Only a child's father conveys citizenship, regardless of the child's country of birth or mother's citizenship. Birth within the country's borders does not confer citizenship, except when a child is born to unknown parents. The law requires that all births be registered within 15 days.

Education: Although primary schooling until age 11 is free and compulsory for all, the media and other sources reported lower enrollment in rural areas, especially for girls. According to 2012 UN statistics, the ratio of girls to boys in primary and secondary school is 98 percent. UNHCR stated that school enrollment among refugees was generally higher outside camps and settlements, where greater resources were available. According to NGO reports presented to the UN Committee on the Rights of the Child, a girl can be denied education if she is pregnant or if her husband so wishes.

<u>Child Abuse</u>: There was little information available to reflect how the government dealt with child abuse, which was largely regarded as a private family matter. The 2002 Law for the Protection of Children and Juvenile states, "Any form of abuse of children and juveniles that causes physical, psychological, or moral harm and threatens their physical or mental health is prohibited," and such crimes carry a maximum sentence of three months or 10 million rials ($332). The law does not directly address sexual molestation nor provide punishment for it.

In October media reported the alleged rape of juvenile, male religious students by renowned Quran reciter, Mohammad Gandom Toosi. According to reports senior regime figures including Supreme Leader Khamenei attempted to cover up the scandal for four years when the victims and their families filed complaints with the judiciary. Toosi denied the charges, and the judiciary has claimed it is difficult to ascertain the truth in such cases. Journalists have been warned against publicizing the ongoing investigation. While no separate law exists for the rape of a child, the crime of rape, regardless of the victim's ages, is potentially punishable by death under the country's Islamic Penal Code.

Despite UN calls for their reopening, the Association for the Defense of Working and Street Children, closed in 2008, and the Society for Endeavoring to Achieve a World Worthy of Children, closed in 2009, remained closed at year's end. The law permits executions of individuals who have reached the age of criminal maturity, defined as age nine for girls and age 13 for boys, if a judge determines the individual understood the nature and consequences of the crime. According to AI at least 160 juveniles were at risk of execution, and authorities executed one individual during the year for alleged crimes committed under the age of 18 (see section 1.a.).

<u>Early and Forced Marriage</u>: The legal minimum age of marriage for girls is 13, but girls as young as nine years old may be married with permission from the court and their father. UNICEF's state of the child report for 2015 estimates 3 percent of girls are married before the age of 15 and 17 percent before the age of 18. UN Committee on the Rights of the Child noted in January that the country continued to maintain practices of child marriage and forced marriage, including thousands of marriages of children below 13 years old.

NGOs reported that many girls committed suicide to escape such marriages and that there were major shortcomings in the country's legal system that "allows sexual intercourse with girls as young as nine lunar years and that other forms of sexual abuse of even younger children is not criminalized." The law requires court approval for the marriage of boys younger than 15 years old. Iran's 2011 national census recorded 11,289 married girls under the age of 18 had at least one child before their 15th birthdays. According to the newspaper *Shahrvand*, there were more than 40,000 registered marriages for girls under the age of 15 in 2014. The number may be higher because NGOs reported that many families did not register underage marriages. Local media reported on a mass marriage ceremony of 50 high school students in Parsian in February where the local governor congratulated the families with gifts.

Female Genital Mutilation/Cutting: See women's section above.

Sexual Exploitation of Children: The legal age requirements for consensual sex are the same as those for marriage, and sex outside of marriage is illegal. The law prohibits all forms of pornography, including child pornography. There are no specific laws regarding child sexual exploitation with such crimes either falling under the category of child abuse or sexual crimes of adultery. According to ICHRI, the legal ambiguity between child abuse and sexual molestation can lead to child sexual molestation cases being prosecuted under adultery laws. Local media reported a sexual abuse case of a nine-year-old girl, Neda, in May who had been sexually abused by her teacher at the 22 Bahman School in Zanjan. Despite medical reports indicating that the teacher had raped the child, ICHRI reported that the court gave the teacher a lesser sentence of having "illegitimate relations."

Displaced Children: There were thousands of Afghan refugee children in the country, many of whom were born in the country but could not obtain identification documents. These children were often unable to attend schools or access basic government services and were vulnerable to labor exploitation and trafficking. In its January commission report, the UN Committee on the Rights of the Child noted continued "allegations of abuse and ill-treatment of refugee and asylum-seeking children by police and security forces."

International Child Abductions: The country is not a party to the 1980 Hague Convention on the Civil Aspects of International Child Abduction. For country-specific information, see the Department of State's website at travel.state.gov/content/childabduction/en/legal/compliance.html.

Anti-Semitism

The law recognizes Jews as a religious minority and provides representation in parliament. Siamak Moreh Sedgh is the Jewish Member of Parliament.

Officials continued to question the history of the Holocaust, and anti-Semitism remained a pervasive problem. A cultural institute organized a third international Holocaust cartoon contest in May (authorities held the first in 2005 and the second in 2015).

Trafficking in Persons

See the Department of State's *Trafficking in Persons Report* at www.state.gov/j/tip/rls/tiprpt/.

Persons with Disabilities

The law generally prohibits discrimination by government actors against persons with disabilities but the law does not apply to private actors. No information was available regarding authorities' effectiveness in enforcing the law. Electoral law prohibits those with visual, hearing, or speech disabilities from running for seats in parliament. While the law provides for government-funded vocational education for persons with disabilities, according to domestic news reports, vocational centers were located in urban areas and unable to meet the needs of the entire population.

The State Welfare Organization of Iran, under the Ministry of Cooperation, Labor, and Social Welfare, is the principal governmental agency charged with protecting the rights of persons with disabilities. It was founded in 1980 to assist persons with disabilities and disadvantaged persons financially and through support to 16 government entities. In addition to supporting low-income groups, it is charged with trying to prevent physical disabilities and support rehabilitation.

The law provides for public accessibility to government-funded buildings, and new structures appeared to comply with the standards in these provisions. There were efforts to increase the access of persons with disabilities to historical sites. Government buildings that predated existing accessibility standards remained largely inaccessible, and general building accessibility for persons with disabilities remained a problem. Persons with disabilities had limited access to informational, educational, and community activities.

National/Racial/Ethnic Minorities

While the constitution grants equal rights to all ethnic minorities and allows minority languages to be used in the media, minorities did not enjoy equal rights, and the government consistently barred the use of their languages in school as the language of instruction. IRGC forces allegedly controlled security in two provinces, Sistan-va Baluchistan and Kurdistan, home to large ethnic minority Baluch and Kurdish communities, respectively.

The government disproportionately targeted minority groups, including Kurds, Ahvazis, Azeris, and Baluchis, for arbitrary arrest, prolonged detention, and physical abuse. UN Committee on Rights of Child reported "widespread discrimination against children of ethnic minorities," as well as "reported targeted arrests, detentions, imprisonments, killings, torture and executions against such groups by the law enforcement and judicial authorities" in its January panel review on the country. These groups reported political and socioeconomic discrimination, particularly in their access to economic aid, business licenses, university admissions, job opportunities, permission to publish books, and housing and land rights. Ethnolinguistic minorities are not free to name their children; the country's civil registry maintains a list of acceptable names, and individuals who wish to choose a name not on this list (in their own language) cannot register the birth of their child. The law, which requires religious screening and allegiance to the concept of "velayat-e faqih" not found in Sunni Islam, impaired the ability of Sunni (many of whom are also Baluch, Ahvazi, or Kurdish) to integrate into civic life and to work in certain fields.

Human rights organizations observed that the government's application of the death penalty disproportionately affected ethnic minorities. In pretrial detention authorities reportedly repeatedly subjected members of minority ethnicities and religions to more severe physical punishment or torture than other prisoners, regardless of the type of crime for which authorities accused them. In his March report, the UN Special Rapporteur reported the continued indiscriminate, extrajudicial killing of unarmed Kurdish smugglers or border couriers in Kermanshah, Kurdistan, Sistan-va Baluchistan, and West Azerbaijan.

The estimated eight million ethnic Kurds in the country frequently campaigned for greater regional autonomy. The government continued to use security law, media law, and other legislation to arrest and prosecute Kurds for exercising their rights to freedom of expression and association. The government reportedly banned Kurdish-language newspapers, journals, and books and punished publishers, journalists, and writers for opposing and criticizing government policies.

Authorities suppressed legitimate activities of Kurdish NGOs by denying them registration permits or bringing security charges against persons working with such organizations. Authorities did not prohibit the use of Kurdish language, but authorities prohibited most schools from teaching it with the exception of the Kurdish language program at the University of Kurdistan.

There were updates in the case of longtime Kurdish rights activist and journalist Mohammad Sediq Kaboudvand, who was originally arrested in 2007 and sentenced to 10 years in prison for "acting against national security" and "propaganda against the state." ICHRI reported he started a hunger strike on May 8 after his conditional release orders were overturned, and new charges were added to his existing sentence after he spoke out about Kurds fighting in Kobani, Syria.

International human rights observers, including the IHRDC, stated that the country's estimated two million Ahvazi Arabs, representing 110 tribes, faced continued oppression and discrimination. Ahvazi rights activists reported the government continued to confiscate Ahvazi property to use for government project development by refusing to recognize the paper deeds of the local population from the prerevolutionary era. The Iranian state-run news agency Young Journalists Club reported the execution of three ethnic Ahvazis, Ghais Obidawi, Ahmad Obidawi, and Sajjad Balawi on August 17. Iran Human Rights reported that the three were sentenced to death without a fair trial. HRANA reported intelligence forces arrested 16 Ahvazi civilians and raided their houses in Shahrak-e-Hamzeh in Dezfool, Khuzestan, on August 23. Their whereabouts remained unknown at year's end.

Ethnic Azeris, who numbered approximately 13 million, or 16 percent of the population, were more integrated into government and society and included the supreme leader among their numbers. IRNA reported the first inclusion of Azeri language and literature majors in universities on August 15. Azeris reported the government, nevertheless, discriminated against them by prohibiting the Azeri language in schools, harassing Azeri activists or organizers, and changing Azeri geographic names. Media reported that 25 protestors were arrested in June after protests erupted in Azeri areas over the publication of lines of poetry in state media that insulted Azeris. HRANA reported the August 18 arrest of Azeri couple, Jalal Shishvani and Shahnaz Tosi, in East Azerbaijan province for their online activism.

Local and international human rights groups alleged serious economic, legal, and cultural discrimination during the year against the predominantly ethnic Baluchi minority, estimated to be between 1.5 and two million persons. Areas with large

Baluchi populations were severely underdeveloped and had limited access to education, employment, health care, and housing, with Baluchi rights activists reporting that more than 70 percent of the population lives under the poverty line. According to activist reports, during the summer authorities set many houses on fire in villages in the Chahbahar region, destroying person's homes. The law limited Sunni Baluchis' employment opportunities and political participation, which caused them to be underrepresented in government positions. Activists reported that throughout the year, and especially during the month of Moharam, the government sent hundreds of Shia missionaries to areas with large Sunni Baluch populations to try to convert the local population. According to Baluchi rights activists, Baluchi journalists and human rights activists faced arbitrary arrest, physical abuse, and unfair trials. Baluchi rights activists reported that families of those in prison were often pressured to remain silent and threatened with retaliation for speaking out about cases.

Human Rights in Iran website reported on October 19 that MOIS agents arrested Ameneh Issazadeh, a Sunni Baluchi girl from Sirik Township, at her home for criticizing religious ceremonies on social media during the month of Moharam. She contacted her family from a MOIS detention center in Bandar Abbas after several days, but her family was not allowed to see her.

Acts of Violence, Discrimination, and Other Abuses Based on Sexual Orientation and Gender Identity

The penal code criminalizes consensual same-sex sexual activity, which is punishable by death, flogging, or a lesser punishment. The law does not distinguish between consensual and nonconsensual same sex intercourse, and NGOs reported this lack of clarity leads to both the victim and the perpetrator being held criminally liable under the law in cases of assault. The law does not prohibit discrimination based on sexual orientation and gender identity. Security forces harassed, arrested, and detained individuals they suspected of being gay or transgender. In some cases security forces raided houses and monitored internet sites for information on LGBTI persons. Those accused of sodomy often faced summary trials, and evidentiary standards were not always met. Punishment for same-sex sexual activity between men was more severe than between women.

The government censored all materials related to LGBTI issues. Authorities particularly blocked websites or content within sites that discussed LGBTI issues, including the censorship of Wikipedia pages defining LGBTI and other related topics. There were active, unregistered LGBTI NGOs in the country. Hate crime laws or other criminal justice mechanisms did not exist to aid in the prosecution of bias-motivated crimes. International LGBTI NGOs reported that many young gay men faced harassment and abuse from family members, religious figures, school leaders, and community elders.

Those dismissed from mandatory military service due to their sexual orientation received special exemption cards indicating the reason for their dismissal, according to the LGBTI activist group 6Rang. Iranian law requires all male citizens over 18 to serve in the military but exempts gay and transgender men, who are classified as having mental disorders. New military ID cards will list the subsection of the law dictating their exemption on their ID cards, which, according to 6Rang, identifies them as gay or transgender and puts them at risk of physical danger and general discrimination.

The government provided transgender persons financial assistance in the form of grants of up to 45 million rials ($1,454) and loans up to 55 million rials ($1,777) to undergo gender-confirmation surgery. Additionally, the Ministry of Cooperatives, Labor, and Social Welfare requires health insurers to cover the cost of gender-confirmation surgery. Individuals who underwent gender-confirmation surgery may petition a court for new identity documents with corrected gender data, which the government reportedly provided efficiently and transparently. NGOs reported that authorities pressured LGBTI persons to undergo gender-confirmation surgery.

HIV and AIDS Social Stigma

Despite government programs to treat and provide financial and other assistance to persons with HIV/AIDS, international news sources and organizations reported that individuals known to be infected with HIV/AIDS faced widespread societal discrimination, including in schools and workplaces.

Other Societal Violence or Discrimination

There was societal discrimination on linguistic grounds against groups whose native language was not Persian, and on religious grounds against non-Shia persons (see International Religious Freedom Report). The extent of such discrimination, largely at the individual level, was difficult to determine.

Section 7. Worker Rights

a. Freedom of Association and the Right to Collective Bargaining

The constitution provides for freedom of association, but neither the constitution nor labor laws specify trade union rights. The law states that workers may establish an Islamic labor council or a guild at any workplace, but the rights and responsibilities of these organizations fall significantly short of international standards for trade unions. In workplaces where workers have established an Islamic labor council, authorities do not permit any other form of worker representation. The law requires prior authorization for organizing and concluding collective agreements. Strikes are prohibited in all sectors, although private-sector workers may conduct "peaceful" campaigns within the workplace. The law does not apply to establishments with fewer than 10 employees.

Authorities did not respect freedom of association and the right to collective bargaining, and the government did not effectively enforce applicable laws. The government severely restricted freedom of association and interfered in worker attempts to organize. The law does not prohibit antiunion discrimination and does not require reinstatement of workers fired for union activity. Antiunion discrimination occurred, and the government imprisoned, harassed, and restricted the activities of labor activists.

The Interior Ministry, the Ministry of Labor, Cooperatives, and Social Welfare, and the Islamic Information Organization determined labor councils' constitutions, operational rules, and election procedures. Administrative and judicial procedures were lengthy. The Workers' House remained the only officially authorized national labor organization, and its leadership oversaw, granted permits to, and coordinated activities with Islamic labor councils in industrial, agricultural, and service organizations with more than 35 employees. According to the ICHRI, the labor councils, which consisted of representatives of workers and a representative of management, were essentially management-run unions that undermined workers' efforts to maintain independent unions. The councils, nevertheless, sometimes could block layoffs and dismissals. Human rights organizations reported that employers routinely fired labor activists for trade union activities. There was no representative workers' organization for noncitizen workers.

According to international media reports, security forces continued to respond to workers' attempts to organize or conduct strikes with arbitrary arrests and violence. Strikes and worker protests often prompted a heavy police response, and security forces routinely monitored major worksites. According to ICHRI, workers are routinely fired and risk arrest for striking, and labor leaders are charged with national security crimes for trying to organize workers. On October

15, labor activists Jafar Azimazadeh and Shapour Ehsani-Rad were sentenced to 11 years in prison for their trade union work supporting a strike at the Safa Rolling and Pipe Mills Company after 16 months without pay. On January 28, workers from the Khatunabad Copper Complex were arrested for protesting against unpaid wages and layoffs and were released on bail pending trial.

The government continued to arrest and harass members of the country's Teachers Association (see section 2.b.). Kurdistan Teachers Association member, Taher Ghaderzadeh, was sentenced to 91 days' imprisonment in April for "participating in assemblies of teachers," and his case is currently being appealed, according to a May report by the World Organization Against Torture. According to ICHRI teachers' activist and board member of the Iranian Teachers Association, Rassoul Boghdadi, was conditionally released on April 29. He was originally set for release after serving a six year sentence in 2015, but a second sentence was added for an additional three years in prison for "insulting Imam Khomeini and the supreme leader" and "propaganda against the state."

b. Prohibition of Forced or Compulsory Labor

The law prohibits all forms of forced or compulsory labor, but the government did not effectively enforce the law. Conditions indicative of forced labor sometimes occurred in the construction, domestic labor, and agricultural sectors, primarily among adult Afghan men. Family members and others forced children to work. The government made no significant effort to address forced labor during the year.

See also the Department of State's *Trafficking in Persons Report* at www.state.gov/j/tip/rls/tiprpt/.

c. Prohibition of Child Labor and Minimum Age for Employment

The law prohibits employment of minors under the age of 15 and places restrictions on employment of minors under the age of 18, such as prohibiting hard labor or night work. The law does not apply to domestic labor and permits children to work in agriculture and some small businesses from the age of 12. The government did not adequately monitor or enforce laws pertaining to child labor, and child labor remained a serious problem. In its January concluding observations, the UN Committee on the Rights of the Child cited a 2003 law that exempts workshops with fewer than 10 employees from labor regulations, as increasing the risks of economic exploitation of children. It also noted serious concerns with the large number of children employed under hazardous conditions, such as in garbage collection, brick kilns, and industrial workshops, without protective clothing and for very low pay.

There were reportedly significant numbers of children, especially of Afghan descent, working as street vendors in major urban areas. The Committee on the Rights of the Child reported problems with street children in particular being subjected to various forms of economic exploitation, including sexual abuse and exploitation by the public and police officers. Child labor also reportedly was used in the production of carpets. Children worked as beggars, and there were reports that criminals forced some children into begging rings.

d. Discrimination with Respect to Employment and Occupation

The constitution bars discrimination based on race, gender, disability, language, and social status "in conformity with Islamic criteria," but the government did not effectively enforce these prohibitions. According to the constitution, "everyone has the right to choose any occupation he wishes, if it is not contrary to Islam and the public interests, and does not infringe the rights of others."

Despite this constitutional provision, the government made systematic efforts to limit women's access to the workplace. In 2015 the Interior Ministry issued an order requiring all officials to hire only secretaries of their own gender. Women remained banned from working in coffee houses and from performing music alongside men with very limited exceptions made for traditional music. Women in many fields were restricted from working after 9 p.m. Hiring practices often discriminated against women, and the Ministry of Labor, Cooperatives, and Social Welfare guidelines state that men should be given preferential hiring status.

e. Acceptable Conditions of Work

According to the Iranian High Labor Council, the minimum wage is more than 8 million rials (around $259) per month; this figure does not include supplemental allowances for housing, groceries, and child benefits. The minimum wage represented a 14 percent increase in 2015; it did not keep pace with inflation, which was estimated at 35 percent for the same year, according to the Central Bank of Iran. Domestic labor organizations published reports stating workers' purchasing power eroded during the past few years as yearly increases in the minimum wage did not kept pace with inflation.

The law establishes a maximum six-day, 44-hour workweek with a weekly rest day, at least 12 days of paid annual leave, and several paid public holidays. Any hours worked above that amount entitles a worker to overtime. The law mandates a payment above the hourly wage to employees for any accrued overtime. The law provides that overtime work is not compulsory. The law does not cover workers in workplaces with fewer than 10 workers, nor does it apply to noncitizens. Employers sometimes subjected migrant workers, most often Afghans, to abusive working conditions, including below-minimum wage salaries, nonpayment of wages, compulsory overtime, and summary deportation without access to food, water, or sanitation facilities during the deportation process.

Many workers continued to be employed on temporary contracts under which they lacked protections available to full-time, noncontract workers and could be dismissed at any time without cause. Large numbers of workers employed in small workplaces or in the informal economy similarly lacked basic protections. Low wages, nonpayment of wages, and lack of job security due to contracting practices continued to be major drivers for strikes and protests.

Little information was available regarding labor inspection and labor law enforcement. While the law provides for occupational health and safety standards, the government sometimes did not enforce these standards in the formal and informal sectors. Labor organizations alleged that hazardous work environments resulted in the deaths of thousands of workers annually. Local media reported on a September 25 cement factory accident that killed one worker and injured others. Iran Human Rights reported that workplace deaths continued to be common throughout the year. Workers do not have the right to remove themselves from situations that endangered their health or safety without jeopardizing their employment.